TED WILLIAMS BIOGRAPHY FOR KIDS

The Inspiring Story of the Greatest Hitter in History

MICHAEL RIDDLE

Copyright © 2025 by Michael Riddle

All rights reserved. The content of this publication may not be reproduced, distributed, or transmitted in any form or by any means, including photocopying, recording, or other electronic or mechanical methods, without the prior written permission of the publisher, except for brief quotations incorporated into critical reviews and specific noncommercial uses allowed by copyright law.

Table of Contents

Introduction..4
Chapter 1: Early Life and Childhood...........................7
Chapter 2: Chasing the Baseball Dream................... 12
Chapter 3: The Splendid Splinter: Rise to Stardom 19
Chapter 4: Ted's Time in the Military........................ 25
Chapter 5: Back to Baseball: Breaking Records..... 32
Chapter 6: Life Beyond the Diamond........................39
Chapter 7: Ted's Greatest Lessons for Kids............ 46
Chapter 8: Fun Facts About Ted Williams................ 52
Quiz Time! Quiz Time!!...56

Introduction

Close your eyes for a moment and imagine this: a young boy standing on a dusty baseball field, gripping a bat that feels just a little too big for him. His heart is racing, his eyes are focused, and he's dreaming big. That boy was Ted Williams, and he had one goal that made his heart soar—to become the greatest hitter in baseball history. Doesn't that sound amazing?

Ted wasn't born famous, and he didn't have any special powers. He was just like you, a kid with dreams and a whole lot of determination. Ted didn't have fancy equipment or a big cheering crowd while growing up. But what he did have was a love for baseball so strong it lit a fire in his heart. He practiced every chance he got—swinging his bat over and over, even when his arms were tired, and chasing fly balls under the hot sun.

Do you know what made Ted different from everyone else? He never gave up. Even when things got hard, when the game seemed tough, or when others doubted him, Ted kept pushing forward. He believed that with enough hard work and focus, he could make his dream come true. And guess what? He did!

Ted Williams became a name that people cheered for all over the world. He could hit baseballs so perfectly that they seemed to fly into the sky like shooting stars. His batting skills amazed fans, his dedication inspired his teammates, and his story has been told for generations. But Ted's journey isn't just about winning games or breaking records. It's about showing that anything is possible if you believe in yourself, work hard, and never let go of your dreams.

As you read this book, you'll step into Ted's shoes and feel the excitement of his incredible journey. You'll learn how he turned a simple love for baseball into a story that still inspires kids today. You'll cheer for him as he hits home runs, admire him as he faces challenges, and discover the amazing lessons he left behind for all of us.

So get ready for a story filled with heart, hard work, and home runs. Ted Williams' life is a reminder that even the biggest dreams can come true if you're willing to chase them. Turn the page, and let's step onto the field with the Splendid Splinter—his story is waiting for you!

Chapter 1: Early Life and Childhood

Ted Williams was born on a warm summer day, August 30, 1918, in sunny San Diego, California. San Diego was a peaceful place back then, filled with tall palm trees, soft sandy beaches, and warm breezes that made it feel like the perfect spot for any little boy to dream big. Ted's family didn't have much money, but that didn't stop him from having a childhood full of imagination and adventure.

Ted's dad, Samuel, worked as a photographer. He was a quiet man who spent a lot of time capturing pictures of families and special moments. Ted's mom, May, was full of energy and always busy helping people through the Salvation Army. She believed in making the world a better place and spent most of her days feeding the hungry and helping the poor. While Ted respected how hard his parents worked, their busy lives often left him with plenty of time to find his own fun.

Ted's love for baseball started when he was very young. He didn't have fancy toys or gadgets, but he had something better—a ball, a bat, and a big dream. In his neighborhood, there were dusty fields where kids would gather to play baseball. Ted was just a little boy, but he would watch the older kids swing the bat and throw the ball. He wanted to be just like them.

At first, Ted wasn't very good. His swings would miss, and when he tried to catch the ball, it would slip right past his glove. But Ted wasn't the kind of kid to give up. He practiced every single day. If he didn't have a baseball, he'd find something else to use, like a rolled-up sock or even a bottle cap. If there wasn't anyone to pitch to him, he'd throw the ball against a wall and practice hitting it when it bounced back.

Ted's family didn't have a lot of money, so he had to be creative. When he couldn't afford a proper bat, he'd use a broomstick. He'd swing it over and over, pretending to be in the middle of a big game. In his mind, the crowd was cheering, the bases were loaded, and it was all up to him to win the game. His imagination turned every practice into an exciting adventure.

At school, Ted wasn't the strongest or the fastest, but he was determined. While other kids played for fun, Ted played to learn. He watched how the best players stood at the plate, how they gripped the bat, and how they swung with power. Then he'd go home and try to copy them. He even set up a mirror so he could watch his swing and make it better.

As Ted grew older, his skills started to improve. By the time he reached high school, he was already a standout player. He joined the baseball team at Herbert Hoover High School, where he became the team's star hitter. Coaches quickly noticed his talent and his incredible focus. Ted wasn't just good; he was determined to be the best.

Even though Ted loved baseball, his family life wasn't always easy. His mom spent so much time helping others that she wasn't home very often. Ted sometimes felt lonely, but he poured all his energy into baseball. It became his escape, his happy place where nothing else mattered.

Ted's hard work didn't go unnoticed. Scouts from professional baseball teams began to hear about the talented kid from San Diego. They were impressed by his powerful swing and his ability to hit the ball with such precision. One day, a scout from the Boston Red Sox came to watch Ted play. He saw something special in the skinny teenager and knew Ted had the potential to be a star.

But Ted wasn't ready to leave his hometown just yet. Instead, he joined a local minor league team called the San Diego Padres. Playing for the Padres was a big deal for Ted. It was his first taste of professional baseball, and he was determined to make the most of it.

Ted worked harder than ever, spending hours on the field practicing his swing. He didn't just want to be good; he wanted to be great. He dreamed of one day playing in the major leagues, standing on the field with the best players in the world.

Looking back, it's amazing to think how far Ted came from those early days in San Diego. He wasn't born a superstar. He didn't have fancy equipment or special training. What he did have was a dream and the determination to chase it. Ted's early life teaches us that even the biggest dreams can start small—with a ball, a bat, and a lot of heart.

This little boy from San Diego, who once practiced with a broomstick and bottle caps, would grow up to become one of the greatest baseball players of all time. And it all started in those dusty fields, where he learned that hard work and determination could make anything possible.

Chapter 2: Chasing the Baseball Dream

Ted Williams' baseball dream grew bigger every single day. By the time he started high school, everyone around him could see how much he loved the game. At Herbert Hoover High School in San Diego, Ted joined the baseball team, and it didn't take long for him to become their best hitter. His teammates would watch in awe as he sent baseballs flying into the outfield, often landing far beyond where anyone expected. Even so, Ted didn't let the attention go to his head. He stayed humble and worked harder than ever.

Ted's days were packed with school, practice, and more practice. After team practices, while most of his friends headed home to relax, Ted would stay behind, swinging his bat over and over again. He wasn't just trying to hit the ball—he was trying to perfect every single swing. If he wasn't happy with how he performed, he'd keep practicing until he got it right. Ted believed that hard work was the key to becoming great, and he wasn't afraid to put in the hours.

But even with all his talent and determination, things weren't always easy for Ted. He didn't have the best equipment or the fanciest gear. His family didn't have the money to buy new baseball gloves or bats, so he had to make do with what he had. Sometimes, Ted borrowed equipment from teammates or repaired old gear to keep playing. Instead of feeling discouraged, he used these challenges as motivation to prove himself.

Ted also faced tough competition from other players who wanted the same thing he did—a shot at the big leagues. There were moments when he struck out or made mistakes on the field, and it frustrated him deeply. But every time something went wrong, Ted reminded himself that even the best players started out as beginners. He didn't let his mistakes hold him back; he used them as lessons to get better.

By the time Ted was finishing high school, people in the baseball world were starting to take notice. Word spread about the skinny kid from San Diego who could hit the ball like no one else. Scouts—people whose job it was to find talented players for professional teams—began showing up to his games. They watched Ted closely, scribbling notes about his powerful swing and incredible focus.

One of the first teams to show interest in Ted was the San Diego Padres, a minor league team. For Ted, this was a dream come true. Playing for the Padres meant he could take his first step toward becoming a professional baseball player while staying close to home. He signed with the team and quickly became one of their standout players. But even though he was thrilled to be playing for the Padres, Ted's ultimate goal was still the major leagues. He wanted to play against the best of the best and prove that he belonged on the biggest stage in baseball.

Ted's time with the Padres was both exciting and challenging. The competition was tougher than anything he had faced before, and the pressure to perform was enormous. Ted had to work harder than ever to keep up with the other players, many of whom were older and more experienced. But instead of feeling intimidated, Ted used this as an opportunity to learn. He studied the game carefully, watching how the best hitters approached each pitch and how they adjusted their swings.

One day, something extraordinary happened. A scout from the Boston Red Sox—a major league team—came to watch Ted play. The scout was amazed by Ted's talent and could see that he had the potential to be a star. After the game, the scout approached Ted and told him that the Red Sox were interested in signing him. Ted could hardly believe what he was hearing. This was the moment he had been dreaming of since he was a little boy practicing with a broomstick and bottle caps.

When Ted officially signed with the Boston Red Sox, it felt like the start of an incredible adventure. He packed up his things and left San Diego, heading to the East Coast to join the team. It was a big change for Ted—he was leaving behind his family, friends, and the city he had always called home. But he was also stepping into a new world filled with exciting possibilities.

Ted's early days with the Red Sox were a mix of excitement and nerves. He was surrounded by some of the best players in the world, and he knew he had a lot to prove. The games were faster, the pitchers were tougher, and the crowds were bigger than anything he had ever experienced. But Ted didn't let that scare him. He reminded himself of all the hard work he had put in over the years and focused on doing his best.

In his first few games with the Red Sox, Ted showed everyone exactly why he had been signed. His powerful swing and ability to hit the ball with precision quickly made him a fan favorite. The crowd would cheer loudly every time Ted stepped up to the plate, and he didn't disappoint. Whether he was hitting home runs or driving in runs with solid base hits, Ted proved that he was ready for the big leagues.

But Ted's journey was far from over. He knew that staying at the top would require even more hard work and dedication. He spent countless hours practicing, studying the game, and improving his skills. Ted didn't just want to be good—he wanted to be the best.

Looking back, Ted's journey to the major leagues was a true testament to his determination and love for the game. He faced challenges, made sacrifices, and worked harder than anyone else to achieve his dream. From his high school days in San Diego to his early success with the Boston Red Sox, Ted's story shows that with passion and perseverance, anything is possible.

And so, Ted Williams began his incredible career as a professional baseball player, ready to take on the world and make his mark on the sport he loved so much. Little did anyone know, this was just the beginning of a journey that would turn him into one of the greatest players in baseball history.

Chapter 3: The Splendid Splinter: Rise to Stardom

Ted Williams wasn't just good at baseball—he was incredible. So incredible, in fact, that people started calling him "The Splendid Splinter." It was a nickname that stuck because of his tall, lean frame and his amazing ability to hit the ball like nobody else could. But Ted's rise to stardom didn't happen overnight. It took years of hard work, practice, and a determination so strong that nothing could stop him.

When Ted joined the Boston Red Sox, he was just a young player with a big dream. He wanted to be the best hitter in baseball, and he wasn't shy about saying so. Some people might have thought he was bragging, but Ted wasn't just talking—he was ready to back it up with his actions. From the moment he stepped onto the field, it was clear that Ted had something special. His swing was smooth and powerful, like poetry in motion. It wasn't just luck, though. Ted had spent years perfecting that swing, practicing until every movement felt natural and precise.

One of the things that set Ted apart was his incredible focus. When he stood at the plate, it was as if the entire world disappeared. All he saw was the ball coming toward him, and he had an uncanny ability to predict exactly where it would go. Pitchers would try their best to trick him with curveballs, fastballs, and sliders, but Ted had an answer for every pitch. He studied pitchers carefully, learning their habits and figuring out how to hit even their trickiest throws.

In 1941, something extraordinary happened—Ted Williams had a season that would go down in history. That year, he became the last player in Major League Baseball to hit over .400 for an entire season. For those who don't know, hitting .400 means getting a hit four out of every ten times at bat. That might not sound like much, but in baseball, it's almost impossible. Most players are lucky to hit .300, so hitting .400 was like climbing Mount Everest—it was a feat of incredible skill and determination.

Ted's .406 batting average in 1941 was the result of his relentless dedication. He didn't just rely on his natural talent; he worked harder than anyone else. He spent hours in the batting cage, practicing his swing until it was perfect. He studied every pitch he faced, breaking down the game in a way that few players ever could. Ted treated baseball like a science, analyzing every detail to make himself better.

But achieving that .406 season wasn't easy. As the season went on and his batting average stayed high, people started to take notice. Reporters wrote articles about his incredible performance, and fans flocked to games just to see him play. By the final day of the season, Ted's batting average was just above .400, and everyone was wondering if he could keep it there.

The Red Sox had a doubleheader that day—two games back-to-back. If Ted wanted to protect his .400 average, he could have chosen to sit out the games. But that wasn't who Ted was. He didn't want to back into history; he wanted to earn it. So, he stepped up to the plate and played both games. And guess what? Ted didn't just protect his .400 average—he raised it to .406! By the end of the day, he had gone 6-for-8, a performance that cemented his place in baseball history.

Ted's achievements made him a hero to fans everywhere. People couldn't get enough of "The Splendid Splinter" and his incredible talent. Kids wanted to be just like him, practicing their swings in the backyard and dreaming of hitting like Ted. Adults admired his dedication and work ethic, seeing him as a symbol of what it meant to strive for greatness.

But Ted's rise to stardom wasn't just about numbers and records. It was about his love for the game and his unwavering determination to be the best. Ted didn't just want to win—he wanted to play the game the right way, with passion and respect. He believed in giving his all, no matter the circumstances. Whether it was a regular season game or the final inning of the World Series, Ted approached every at-bat with the same level of intensity and focus.

Ted's hard work didn't stop at the plate. He was also an excellent outfielder, known for his strong arm and ability to track down fly balls. While most people remember him for his hitting, Ted was a complete player who could impact the game in many ways.

Even as Ted became one of the most famous players in baseball, he never forgot where he came from. He often talked about his early days in San Diego, practicing with a broomstick and bottle caps. Those humble beginnings shaped who he was and reminded him of the importance of hard work and perseverance.

Ted Williams' rise to stardom is a story of grit, determination, and an unshakable belief in his own abilities. He didn't let challenges or setbacks stop him from chasing his dreams, and his dedication paid off in ways that continue to inspire people to this day. From his

.406 season to his countless other achievements, Ted proved that with passion and effort, anything is possible.

For young baseball fans, Ted's story is a reminder that greatness isn't something you're born with—it's something you earn. It's about showing up every day, working hard, and believing in yourself, even when things get tough. Ted Williams wasn't just a baseball player; he was a symbol of what it means to dream big and work hard to make those dreams come true. And that's what makes his story so special.

Chapter 4: Ted's Time in the Military

Ted Williams' journey to becoming a baseball legend took an unexpected turn during the prime of his career. He was at the top of his game, with his bat swinging mightily and his name on everyone's lips, when the country called on him to serve. It was the time of World War II, and like many others, Ted knew that his country needed him. So, he put down his bat and glove and picked up something entirely different: a military uniform.

Ted didn't have to go to war—many baseball players were allowed to continue playing while the world was at war. But Ted believed in doing his part. He didn't want to sit on the sidelines while others were fighting for their country. Ted's decision wasn't easy. Baseball was his passion, and he had worked so hard to get where he was. But deep down, he knew that serving his country was something bigger than baseball, something he couldn't ignore.

In 1943, at the height of his career, Ted enlisted in the U.S. Navy. He was eager to do whatever was needed. Ted didn't just join the military to wear the uniform; he wanted to contribute in any way he could. And so, he began training to become a fighter pilot. At the time, not everyone knew it, but Ted was a natural when it came to flying. He quickly proved that he was an excellent pilot, mastering the skills needed to fly complex aircraft. For someone who had spent so much time perfecting his baseball swing, learning to control a fighter plane came with its own challenges. But Ted's determination was evident as he embraced the challenge.

It was a huge change for Ted. Instead of being surrounded by teammates, he was now part of a different kind of team, one that flew in the skies to protect their country. He was no longer just Ted Williams, the baseball star—he was now Ted Williams, a member of the military who was ready to fight for freedom. The work was difficult, and there were times when Ted missed his life on the baseball field, but he was proud of what he was doing. Ted's bravery and commitment to his country showed the world that even a famous baseball player could put aside personal success to serve the greater good.

Ted spent time flying combat missions during World War II, and though he never saw combat directly, he was still risking his life every time he flew. His military service wasn't just about fighting battles in the sky—it was about showing up when needed and doing his duty, no matter the personal cost. After World War II ended, Ted returned home and rejoined the Red Sox, but his service wasn't over yet. Just a few years later, when the Korean War broke out in 1950, Ted was called back into service. Once again, he put down his bat and picked up a uniform, ready to serve his country.

Ted flew more combat missions during the Korean War, this time as a pilot in the Marine Corps. The decision to return to war wasn't an easy one for Ted. Baseball was calling him back, and he was in the prime of his career. But just like during World War II, Ted knew that some things were more important than baseball. He was determined to do his part, no matter how tough it might be.

Flying over the skies of Korea wasn't easy. The missions were dangerous, and the risks were high. But Ted, with his incredible focus and steady hand, flew those missions like a true hero. Despite the pressures of being a baseball legend, Ted was determined to be just as good a pilot as he was a hitter. He learned more about discipline, courage, and leadership during his time in the military than he could have ever imagined.

Though his time away from baseball was a sacrifice, it taught Ted Williams lessons that would stick with him for the rest of his life. The biggest lesson he learned from his military service wasn't how to fly a plane or fight in a war—it was about putting others before himself. Ted learned that sometimes doing the right thing means making tough choices and sacrifices. He could have stayed home and played baseball, but he chose to be a part of something bigger than himself. And in doing so, he showed the world what true courage and honor looked like.

After his time in the military, Ted returned to baseball again, but his experience shaped him in ways he hadn't expected. He brought with him a new perspective on life and on the game he loved. His military service had given him a sense of discipline and resilience that would help him face even the toughest moments in his baseball career. He was a man who had faced adversity and come out stronger on the other side.

Ted's time in the military also taught him the importance of teamwork. In the military, every mission was a team effort, and no one could succeed alone. It was the same in baseball. Ted realized that while he was the star of the team, the team needed every player to work together to achieve their goals. He came back to baseball with a renewed sense of respect for his teammates and the role they played in his success.

Through his service, Ted Williams also learned how to balance his responsibilities. Baseball was still a huge part of his life, but he had also experienced something that gave him perspective: a bigger purpose. It wasn't just about being a great baseball player anymore; it was about understanding that there was more to life than just personal success. Ted had seen firsthand the sacrifices people made, and he knew that life wasn't always going to be about what he wanted. Sometimes, it was about doing the right thing, even if it wasn't the easiest path.

Ted's story from the battlefield to the baseball diamond is one of courage, commitment, and sacrifice. It teaches us that being a hero isn't always about wearing a cape or hitting home runs—it's about doing what's right when the stakes are high. Ted Williams wasn't just a legend on the field; he was a hero who served his country with honor, and his time in the military was just as important as his time in the major leagues.

Looking back on his life, Ted knew that his time in the military helped shape the man he became. It taught him life lessons that he carried with him both on and off the field. Ted's service gave him a new appreciation for the people who work hard behind the scenes, the ones who don't get the spotlight but who play a crucial role in the success of something bigger than themselves. It made him humble, and it gave him a sense of responsibility that he carried through the rest of his career and life.

Chapter 5: Back to Baseball: Breaking Records

Ted Williams had already achieved so much before he left for war, but when he came back to baseball, it was like he was starting a new chapter in an already amazing story. His time in the military had changed him, and now he was ready to return to the sport he loved, more determined than ever. When Ted returned to the Boston Red Sox in 1946 after his military service, it didn't take long for fans to see that he was just as good as he'd ever been—and maybe even better.

At first, people were worried. Could the great Ted Williams still hit like he used to? After all, he'd been away from the game for a few years. Would he be rusty? Would he be able to catch up with all the young, talented players who had emerged during his time away? The answer came quickly. Ted stepped up to the plate, and it was like he had never left. He was still the same incredible hitter, still the same Splendid Splinter, and still able to do things that amazed everyone.

In his first full season back in 1946, Ted Williams didn't just come back—he came back with a bang. He led the Red Sox to the World Series that year, and though they didn't win the championship, Ted proved that he was still the best hitter in the game. He finished the season with a batting average of .342, which is amazing by itself, but what really stood out was how quickly he got back into form after so much time away. Ted was on a mission to prove that nothing could stop him, and he was doing it every time he stepped up to the plate.

But Ted's story didn't stop there. He wasn't just a player who came back from war and kept playing. He was a player who came back and shattered records. His return to the game was filled with historic home runs, batting titles, and All-Star moments that made him even more of a legend than he had been before.

One of the most unforgettable moments in Ted Williams' career happened in 1947 when he hit his 500th career home run. It was a huge milestone, and it solidified Ted's place as one of the greatest players to ever play the game. Ted's home runs weren't just impressive because of the number, though—they were impressive because of the way he hit them. Ted had a natural swing that seemed effortless, but it was incredibly powerful. When he hit a home run, it wasn't just a long ball—it was a statement. Ted could hit the ball farther and harder than most players, and every time he sent one flying over the fence, fans would hold their breath and watch in awe.

Ted didn't just hit home runs. He also led the league in batting average multiple times after returning from the war. In 1948, for example, he won the American League batting title with a .369 batting average. That's an incredible number, and it's a reminder of just how amazing Ted was at the plate. Even after all the years away from the game, Ted was still able to hit better than most players in the league. He was a true master of the art of hitting.

But Ted didn't just set individual records—he also helped his team succeed. He was an All-Star almost every season after his return from the military, making his mark not only as one of the best hitters of his time but also as one of the most important players in the league. Ted's influence on his teammates was enormous. He was known for his intense focus and his unrelenting drive to be the best, and his work ethic inspired those around him to push themselves just as hard.

The Red Sox benefited from Ted's return in a big way. He was a leader both on and off the field, showing everyone how to work hard and never give up. Ted didn't just play the game—he made everyone around him better. His presence in the clubhouse and on the field lifted the entire team to new heights, and while the Red Sox didn't win the World Series during Ted's second stint with the team, his impact was felt for years.

Ted Williams wasn't just a hero to the fans of the Boston Red Sox. He was a hero to baseball fans everywhere. His dedication to the game was unmatched, and his return to baseball after serving in two wars only made him more admired. Fans from all over the country would watch him play, hoping to see one of his legendary home runs or witness the magic of his swing. It wasn't just about numbers—it was about the excitement of watching one of the greatest players to ever play the game.

As the years went by, Ted continued to make history. In 1957, he became the oldest player ever to win a batting title at the age of 39. But even as he got older, Ted didn't lose his ability to perform at the highest level. He proved that age wasn't a barrier to greatness. It didn't matter how old he got—he was still Ted Williams, and he was still going to hit better than most players out there.

Ted's playing style, with his smooth, powerful swing, became a model for future generations. Young players watched him closely, trying to learn from the best. Ted's swing was a thing of beauty, and many young hitters wanted to copy it. It wasn't just about mimicking his movements, though. Ted taught young players that hitting was about more than just physical ability. It was about understanding the game, studying the pitchers, and putting in the work to perfect your craft. Ted was a true student of the game, and he passed that knowledge down to the next generation of players.

Even after Ted Williams retired from baseball in 1960, his influence continued to be felt. He had set a new standard for what it meant to be a great hitter. Players like Tony Gwynn, Wade Boggs, and others who followed in Ted's footsteps learned from his example. Ted's dedication to his craft, his ability to hit, and his passion for the game were all part of the legacy he left behind.

Ted's return to baseball after serving in the military wasn't just about breaking records—it was about showing the world what it meant to be a true champion. He came back stronger than ever, with the same focus and dedication that had made him one of the greatest players in the history of the game. Through his historic home runs, batting titles, and All-Star moments, Ted Williams proved that no matter what challenges life throws your way, you can always come back and do something amazing.

And that's exactly what Ted Williams did. He didn't just return to baseball—he returned and set new standards, broke new records, and inspired countless young players to strive for greatness. He showed them that greatness wasn't just about talent—it was about hard work, perseverance, and a love for the game. Ted Williams didn't just play baseball; he changed the way we think about what it means to be a true legend.

Chapter 6: Life Beyond the Diamond

Ted Williams was one of the greatest baseball players to ever live, but even legends have to hang up their gloves and cleats at some point. After an incredible career, Ted retired from playing baseball in 1960. It was a bittersweet moment for fans who had watched him hit home runs and achieve greatness on the field for so many years. But Ted's story didn't end when he walked away from baseball; in fact, it was just the beginning of another exciting chapter in his life.

When Ted Williams retired from playing baseball, it didn't mean that he was done with the sport entirely. In fact, he stayed involved in baseball in many ways. One of the things Ted loved most about the game was helping young players learn and grow. After retiring from the major leagues, Ted spent some time working as a manager. This gave him the chance to teach others what he had learned over his long career. Ted didn't just want to be remembered for his amazing batting skills—he wanted to pass on his knowledge to the next generation of players.

As a manager, Ted was known for being tough but fair. He expected hard work from his players, just like he had demanded from himself during his playing days. But he also cared deeply about helping them improve. Ted knew that success in baseball wasn't just about talent—it was about understanding the game and putting in the effort. He spent time teaching young players the skills that had made him great, from the importance of working on their swing to the value of studying pitchers and knowing how to approach every at-bat. Ted wanted the players he mentored to be as successful as possible, and he was always there to offer advice and guidance.

Though Ted loved managing and working with young players, there was one thing that he loved even more: fishing. If you've ever seen a baseball player spend time away from the diamond, you know that many of them have hobbies they enjoy. For Ted Williams, fishing was more than just a hobby—it was a true passion. From the moment he retired, Ted spent as much time as he could fishing in the beautiful waters around Florida. It was a way for him to relax and unwind after years of intense pressure in the spotlight.

Ted's love for fishing was so strong that he even worked as a commercial fisherman for a while. It wasn't just about having fun—it was about the thrill of catching fish and the joy of spending time out on the water. Ted became well-known in the fishing community, not just for his skills with a rod and reel but also for his knowledge of the sport. He became a respected figure in the world of fishing, and he even started his own fishing show on television, where he shared his love for the sport with fans.

But Ted Williams didn't just spend his time fishing and relaxing after retiring. He also worked hard to ensure that his legacy would live on. One of the ways Ted did this was by contributing to the game of baseball in other ways, such as helping to design new equipment and sharing his insights with coaches and players. Ted always believed in improving the game, and he knew that the best way to do that was by continuing to be involved in baseball, even if he wasn't playing anymore. He wanted to make sure that baseball remained the best sport it could be and that young players had the tools and knowledge they needed to succeed.

Even though Ted Williams wasn't playing baseball anymore, he was still a big part of the game. His name was known by baseball fans everywhere, and his legacy continued to grow. Ted's impact on the game was undeniable. From his time with the Boston Red Sox to his incredible accomplishments on the field, Ted had already left a lasting mark on the history of baseball. But it was his work off the field that truly helped to cement his place as one of the greatest players to ever live.

Over the years, Ted received countless honors and awards for his contributions to baseball. He was inducted into the Baseball Hall of Fame in 1966, just a few years after retiring from the game. Being inducted into the Hall of Fame was a huge honor, and it was the perfect way to celebrate his amazing career. But Ted didn't rest on his laurels. He continued to be involved in baseball in the years that followed, whether it was offering advice to young players or supporting charitable causes that helped the sport grow.

Through it all, Ted Williams remained a humble man who loved the game of baseball and cared deeply about passing on his knowledge to others. He believed that the sport had given him so much, and he wanted to make sure that future generations had the same opportunities to enjoy the game. Ted didn't see himself as a hero or a legend. He saw himself as someone who loved baseball and wanted to share that love with the world.

Ted's legacy goes far beyond his records and his amazing accomplishments on the field. It's about the way he inspired others to reach for greatness, the way he taught young players to work hard and always strive for improvement. It's about the way he showed that dedication, hard work, and a love for the game could take you to places you never imagined. Ted Williams didn't just play baseball—he helped shape the future of the sport.

Even in his later years, Ted was a source of inspiration. When he wasn't fishing, mentoring, or contributing to the game he loved, he was spending time with his family. He was a father and a grandfather, and he cared deeply about his loved ones. Ted's life beyond baseball was rich and full, and he continued to make an impact in ways big and small.

Ultimately, Ted Williams is regarded as one of the all-time greats of baseball. But his life wasn't just about baseball—it was about passion, dedication, and sharing that passion with others. Whether he was on the field hitting home runs, teaching young players how to improve, or relaxing with a fishing rod in hand, Ted's legacy continues to live on.

His story reminds us that greatness isn't just about what we achieve—it's about the way we inspire others and the way we share our love for what we do with the world. Ted Williams will always be remembered not just as a baseball player, but as someone who gave everything to the game, to his fans, and to those who followed in his footsteps.

Chapter 7: Ted's Greatest Lessons for Kids

Ted Williams' life is packed with powerful lessons you can carry with you. His journey shows how determination, focus, humility, and hard work can help us overcome challenges and achieve amazing things. By looking at Ted's story, you'll see how his values shaped not only his career but also the way he lived. These lessons can help you face your own challenges, dream big, and keep pushing forward no matter what.

When Ted was a young boy, he didn't always have the easiest start in life, but he knew that if he wanted to succeed, he had to put in the effort. He wasn't born a superstar—he had to work hard every day to become the player we all admire. This is where the lesson of determination comes in. You see, determination is about not giving up when things get tough. It's about setting a goal and sticking with it, even when the road gets hard.

Ted faced many challenges—criticism, injury, and even time away from the game for military service. But no matter what, he kept going. He believed in his dream and kept pushing himself to be better every day.

You can learn from Ted's determination. Think about a time when something felt too hard. Maybe you wanted to give up, but instead, you kept trying. That's the spirit Ted had. It didn't matter if he struck out, if he had a bad game, or if people didn't believe in him. He was determined to be the best, and that's why he became one of the greatest baseball players of all time.

Focus was another key part of Ted Williams' success. When Ted was at the plate, he wasn't distracted by anything. The noise of the crowd, the pressure of the game—none of that mattered. He focused entirely on the pitch coming toward him. It wasn't just his talent that made him great; it was his ability to stay locked in and concentrate on the task at hand. This focus helped him hit home runs, win batting titles, and set records that still stand today.

Imagine yourself in a big game, or working on a project at school. How often do you find yourself distracted by thoughts of other things? Ted's ability to block out distractions and focus on the moment is something you can try to do too. When you're focused, you can accomplish so much more. Whether it's finishing homework, practicing a sport, or just talking with a friend, staying focused will help you do your best.

Even with all his success, Ted was known for his humility. He didn't let his achievements make him arrogant or proud. In fact, he treated everyone with respect, no matter who they were. His humility meant that even though he was the best, he never thought of himself as better than anyone else. He believed in treating people well and staying grounded. This lesson of humility is something everyone can take to heart.

You don't have to brag or show off to be respected. Just like Ted, you can be confident in what you do without letting it make you think you're better than others.

Humility means being kind, respectful, and recognizing that everyone has something special to offer. If you stay humble, people will admire you not just for your achievements, but for how you treat others.

Hard work was the foundation of Ted Williams' career. He knew that talent alone wouldn't make him great. He spent countless hours practicing his swing, studying pitchers, and improving his skills. Even though he had natural talent, Ted always believed that hard work was what made him stand out. If he wasn't practicing or playing, he was thinking about how he could get better. He was always striving for perfection, and that dedication paid off.

This lesson is one you can apply in your own life. It's not enough to just have a talent or a skill—you have to work at it. Think about the things you love to do. Whether it's sports, drawing, singing, or anything else, you can get better by practicing and putting in the effort. Ted didn't become a legend by sitting back and waiting for things to happen. He worked hard every day, and you can too.

Ted's life also shows the power of confidence. He believed in himself, even in the toughest times. Ted didn't let failure stop him. He didn't let people's doubts or setbacks shake his confidence. He knew that with enough effort, he could accomplish anything. This is a huge lesson for you. Believing in yourself is important, and confidence doesn't come from being perfect. It comes from knowing that you can handle whatever comes your way and trusting that with enough practice and hard work, you'll reach your goals.

Finally, Ted's story teaches us all about resilience. Life isn't always easy. Ted faced plenty of challenges, from injuries to having to leave the game to serve in the military. But each time, he bounced back stronger. Resilience means picking yourself up after you fall, learning from your mistakes, and never giving up. You can be resilient too. The next time something doesn't go your way, think of Ted and remember that setbacks are just part of the journey.

Ted Williams' greatest lessons can help you not only in baseball but in life. His determination to keep going, focus on what matters, humility in his success, hard work, confidence, and resilience are all things that can help you achieve your goals. Ted's life reminds you that you don't have to be perfect to be great; you just have to keep working, stay focused, and treat others with respect. No matter what you want to do in life, Ted's story shows that anything is possible if you keep pushing forward with heart and effort.

Chapter 8: Fun Facts About Ted Williams

1. The "Splendid Splinter"

Ted Williams was known as the "Splendid Splinter" because of his amazing ability to hit the baseball. His nickname came from the way he could hit the ball so far and hard, even though he wasn't a giant guy. People loved watching him play, and that nickname stuck with him forever!

2. Ted Loved Fishing

After retiring from baseball, Ted spent a lot of time fishing! He loved being out on the water, and he was really good at it. Ted even became a fishing guide and wrote books about his adventures. If you love being outdoors and enjoy fishing, Ted was your guy!

3. Hitting Over .400

In 1941, Ted Williams did something that no one has done since—he finished the season with a .406 batting average! This means that Ted got a hit more than four times out of every 10 times he stepped up to bat. It was an amazing record, and it's still one of the best achievements in baseball!

4. Ted Was Into Science

Ted wasn't just a baseball player—he was also a science lover! He loved learning new things, especially about flying. After his baseball career, Ted became a test pilot and flew new planes. He even wrote about flying and made sure to keep learning, even after becoming a legend on the baseball field.

5. A Special Connection With Fans

Ted Williams might have been a baseball star, but he was also known for being humble. One time, after hitting a big home run, Ted didn't want to take a bow or wave to the crowd. He said he wanted the fans to remember the game, not him! It showed how much he cared about the sport and his fans.

6. The Power of Focus

Ted Williams had a special gift for focusing on his game. One of the most impressive things he did was hit two home runs even when he was recovering from an injury! His focus and determination to keep playing even when it was hard made him stand out as one of the greatest players ever.

7. The Baseball Hall of Fame

Ted Williams was so good at baseball that he was inducted into the Baseball Hall of Fame in 1966. That's a huge honor, and it shows how much people respected him not just for his stats, but for his love of the game and the way he played.

8. He Could Have Played in the NFL

Ted Williams was an amazing athlete, and he could have played other sports too! He was an incredible football player in high school and was even recruited by NFL teams. But Ted chose baseball instead, and that's where he became a legend.

9. A Record-Setting Career

Ted Williams finished his career with 521 home runs, a number that put him among the greatest players of all time. But what made his record even more impressive was that he achieved it while missing several seasons to serve in the military. Imagine what he could have done if he hadn't taken that time off!

10. He Never Got to Play in a World Series

Even though Ted Williams was one of the best players ever, he never got the chance to play in a World Series. It was a big disappointment for him because he always dreamed of winning a championship. But despite not winning a World Series, Ted's incredible career left an unforgettable legacy.

Quiz Time! Quiz Time!!

Are you ready to see how much you remember about the amazing Ted Williams? Let's see if you can score a home run with these fun questions!

1. Where did Ted Williams grow up?

- a) New York

- b) San Diego

- c) Boston

- d) Chicago

2. What was Ted Williams' famous nickname?

- a) The Hit Machine

- b) The Splendid Splinter

- c) The Baseball King

- d) The Bat Master

3. Which Major League Baseball team did Ted Williams play for?

- a) New York Yankees

- b) Boston Red Sox
- c) Chicago Cubs
- d) Los Angeles Dodgers

4. In what year did Ted Williams finish the season with a batting average of .406?
- a) 1940
- b) 1941
- c) 1950
- d) 1951

5. What war did Ted Williams serve in during World War II?
- a) World War I
- b) World War II
- c) Vietnam War
- d) Korean War

6. How many years did Ted Williams miss from baseball because of his military service?
a) 1 year

b) 3 years

c) 5 years

d) 2 years

7. What was Ted Williams' biggest regret in his baseball career?

- a) Never winning a World Series
- b) Not hitting enough home runs
- c) Not retiring earlier
- d) Never being named MVP

8. Which of the following is one of Ted Williams' most famous achievements?

- a) 700 home runs
- b) Batting .406 in a season
- c) Winning 10 World Series rings
- d) Playing for 30 seasons

9. What sport did Ted Williams play as a young boy before he fell in love with baseball?

- a) Basketball
- b) Football

- c) Soccer
- d) Tennis

10. What other job did Ted Williams do besides playing baseball?

a) Scientist

b) Pilot

c) Doctor

d) Teacher

11. How old was Ted Williams when he made his Major League Baseball debut?

- a) 18
- b) 20
- c) 22
- d) 24

12. What was Ted Williams known for besides his batting?

- a) His speed
- b) His powerful pitching arm
- c) His great leadership

- d) His patience and focus at the plate

13. What was Ted Williams' batting average at the end of his career?
- a) .310
- b) .350
- c) .400
- d) .344

14. What was the nickname given to Ted Williams because of his famous hitting ability?
- a) The King of the Bat
- b) The Splendid Splinter
- c) The Babe
- d) The Hitting Machine

15. What did Ted Williams believe was the key to being a successful baseball player?
- a) Strength
- b) Intelligence
- c) Dedication and focus

- d) Luck

Answer Key:

1. b) San Diego
2. b) The Splendid Splinter
3. b) Boston Red Sox
4. b) 1941
5. b) World War II
6. b) 3 years
7. a) Never winning a World Series
8. b) Batting .406 in a season
9. b) Football
10. b) Pilot
11. b) 20
12. d) His patience and focus at the plate
13. d) .344
14. b) The Splendid Splinter
15. c) Dedication and focus

Made in the USA
Las Vegas, NV
09 April 2025